More Stories from the Old Testament
For Children

Matty Robins

For information about permission to reproduce selections from this book, write to Permissions. The Light and the Way Books.

6845 Elm Street, McLean Va. 22101

Visit our Web site: WWW. Litchfield Literary Books.Com

THIS BOOK BELONGS TO_____

"Suffer the little children to come unto me, and forbid them not: for of such is the kingdom of God"

Contents

PREFACE

"The Children's Bible" provides, in simple English, a translation of selections from both the Old and the New Testament. These selections have been made as a result of more than twenty-five years of observation and study. The text is that of the Bible itself, but in the language of the child, so that it may easily be read to the younger children and by those who are older. It is not in words of one syllable, for while the child is reading the Bible he should gradually learn the meaning of new words and idioms.

The Bible contains the foundations on which the religious life of the child must be built. The immortal stories and songs of the Old and New Testaments are his richest inheritance from the past. To give him this heritage in language and form that he can understand and enjoy is the duty and privilege of his parents and teachers.

It is hoped that "The Children's Bible" will meet the need and the demand, which parents and educators alike have long felt and often expressed, for a simple translation of selections from the Bible most suited to the needs and the interests of the child. It is also believed that after the child has learned to appreciate and love these stories and songs, he will be eager and able to read the Bible as a whole with genuine interest and understanding.

THE BOYHOOD AND TRAINING OF MOSES

After the death of Joseph and his brothers, the Israelites increased so rapidly and became so many and powerful that the land was filled with them. But a new king who did not know Joseph ruled over Egypt. He said to his people, "See, the Israelites are becoming too many and powerful for us. Come, let us deal wisely with them, for fear that they become so many that, if war is begun against us, they will join our enemies and fight against us and leave the land."

So the Egyptians set taskmasters over them to put burdens upon them. And they built for Pharaoh the store-cities, Pithom and Rameses. But the more the Egyptians afflicted them, the more numerous they became and the more they spread everywhere, so that the Egyptians dreaded what they might do. And the Egyptians were cruel and made slaves of them, making their lives bitter with hard labor in mortar and brick, and by all kinds of hard work in the field.

Pharaoh also gave this command to all his people, "You shall throw into the river every son that is born to the Hebrews, but every daughter you shall save alive."

Now a man of the tribe of Levi married a woman of the same tribe, and she had a son. When she saw that he was a beautiful child, she hid him for three months. But when she could no longer hide him, she took a basket made of papyrus reeds, daubed it with mortar and pitch, and put the child in it. Then she placed it in the reeds by the bank of the river Nile, while his sister stayed near by to see what would happen to him.

The daughter of Pharaoh came down to bathe in the Nile, and while her maids were walking along the river's bank, she saw the basket among the reeds and sent her waiting-maid to bring it. When she opened it and saw the child, the boy was crying; and she felt sorry for him and said, "This is one of the Hebrew children."

Then his sister said to Pharaoh's daughter, "Shall I go and call one of the Hebrew women to nurse the child for you?" Pharaoh's daughter said to her, "Go." So the maiden went and called the child's mother, and Pharaoh's daughter said to her, "Take this child away and nurse it for me, and I will pay you your wages." Then the woman took the child and nursed it. When the child had grown up, she brought him to Pharaoh's daughter, and he became her son; and she named him Moses, for she said, "I drew him out of the water."

One time, after Moses had grown up, he went out to his own people; andas he was watching them at their hard labor, he saw an Egyptian beating a Hebrew, one of his own race. He looked around and seeing that there was no one in sight, he killed the Egyptian and hid him in the sand.

On the next day Moses went out, and saw two Hebrews struggling together; and he said to the one who was in the wrong, "Why do you strike your fellow workman?" The man replied, "Who made you a ruler and a judge over us? Do you intend to kill me as you killed the Egyptian?" Then Moses was afraid and said, "What I have done is known!" When Pharaoh heard what had taken place, he tried to put Moses to death; but Moses left the country and made his home in the land of Midian.

As he was sitting by a well, the seven daughters of the priest of Midian came and drew water and filled the troughs to water their father's flock, but the shepherds came and drove them away. Then Moses stood up and protected the women and watered their flock.

When they came to their father, he said, "How is it that you have come back so early to-day?" They replied, "An Egyptian protected us from the shepherds, and besides, he drew water for us and watered the flock."

Then he said to his daughters, "Where is he? Why have you left the man? Ask him to eat with us." So Moses made his home with the man; and he gave Moses his daughter Zipporah to be his wife. She had a son, and Moses named him Gershom.

THE VOICE FROM THE BUSH

After a long time the king of Egypt died. Moses was taking care of the flock of Jethro his wife's father. Once he led the flock to the other side of the pasture and came to Horeb, the mountain of God. There the angel of Jehovah appeared to him in a flame of fire from the midst of a thorn bush. As he looked, the bush flamed up without being burned. Moses said, "I will stop here and see this wonderful sight, why the bush is not burned up."

When Jehovah saw that Moses stopped to look, he called to him from the midst of the bush, "Moses, Moses." Moses answered, "Here am I." Then God said, "Do not come near; take your shoes off your feet, for the place where you are standing is holy ground." He also said, "I am the God of your forefathers, the God of Abraham, the God of Isaac, and the God of Jacob." Then Moses covered his face; for he was afraid to look upon God.

But Jehovah said, "I have certainly seen the suffering of my people who are in Egypt and have heard their cry of distress because of their taskmasters, for I know their sorrows. I have come down to rescue them from the power of the Egyptians and to bring them out of that land into a land that is beautiful and wide, to a land with plenty of milk and honey. I have heard the cry of the Israelites and I have seen how they suffer at the hands of the Egyptians. Come now, I will send you to Pharaoh that you may bring my people, the Israelites, out of Egypt."

But Moses said to God, "Who am I, that I should go to Pharaoh and should bring the Israelites out of Egypt?" He answered, "I will surely be with you; and this shall be the sign to you that I have sent you: when you have brought the people out of Egypt, you shall worship God upon this mountain."

Then Moses said to God, "If I go to the Israelites and say to them, 'The God of your forefathers has sent me to you,' and they ask me, 'What is his name?' what shall I answer them?"

God said to Moses, "I AM WHAT I AM"; and he said, "Declare to the Israelites: 'I AM has sent me to you.' Go and gather the leaders of Israel together and say to them, 'Jehovah the God of your forefathers, the God of Abraham, Isaac, and Jacob, has appeared to me and said, I have surely remembered you and have seen what is being done to you in Egypt, and I have declared that I will bring you up out of the suffering in Egypt to a land with plenty of milk and honey.' They will listen to your voice; and you, together with the leaders of Israel, shall go to the king of Egypt and say to him, 'Jehovah, the God of the Hebrews, has appeared to us. Now let us go three days' journey into the wilderness, that we may offer a sacrifice to Jehovah our God.' But I know that the king of Egypt will not let you go unless he is made to do so by a mighty power. Therefore I will use my power and overwhelm Egypt with all the marvellous deeds that I will do there. After that he will let you go."

Moses said to Jehovah, "O, Lord I am not able to speak well; for I am slow to speak and slow in saying what I think."

Jehovah said to him, "Who has given man a mouth? Or who makes one deaf or dumb, or blind or able to see? Is it not I, Jehovah? Now go, and I will be with you and teach you what you shall say; and your brother Aaron shall speak for you to the people."

Then Moses went back to Jethro, his wife's father, and said to him, "Let me go again to my people in Egypt to see whether they are still alive." Jethro answered Moses, "Go, with my blessing."

PHARAOH THE STUBBORN RULER

Then Jehovah said to Aaron, "Go into the wilderness to meet Moses." So he went and met him on the mountain of God and kissed him. And Moses told Aaron all that Jehovah had sent him to declare. So Moses and Aaron gathered all the leaders of the Israelites, and Aaron repeated all the words which Jehovah had spoken to Moses. The people believed; and when they heard that Jehovah had remembered the Israelites and that he had seen their suffering, they bowed their heads and worshipped.

Then Moses and Aaron went to Pharaoh and said to him, "Jehovah, the God of Israel commands, 'Let my people go that they may hold a feast in my honor in the wilderness.'" But Pharaoh said, "Who is Jehovah that I should obey his command to let Israel go? I do not know Jehovah, and I will not let Israel go." They said, "The God of the Hebrews has appeared to us; let us go three days' journey into the wilderness that we may offer a sacrifice to Jehovah our God, that he may not attack us with pestilence or with the sword." But the king of Egypt replied, "Moses and Aaron, why do you try to turn the people from their work? Go to your tasks!"

The same day Pharaoh gave this command to the taskmasters who were over the people: "You shall no longer give the people straw for making bricks as before. Let them go and gather straw for themselves. But you shall demand of them the same number of bricks that they have been making before; you shall not lessen the number at all, for they are lazy; that is why they cry out, 'Let us go and offer a sacrifice to our God.' Let heavier work be laid upon the men, that they may be kept so busy that they will not pay attention to lying words."

So the taskmasters who were over the people went out and said to them, "This is Pharaoh's order, 'I will no longer give you straw. Go yourselves, get straw wherever you can find it; but your work shall not be made less.'" So the people were scattered over all the land of Egypt to gather stubble for straw. The taskmasters urged them on, saying, "You must finish your daily task just as when there was straw." The overseers of the Israelites, whom Pharaoh's taskmasters had put over them, were also beaten and asked, "Why have you not finished to-day as many bricks as yesterday?"

Then the overseers of the Israelites went to Pharaoh and said, "Why do you deal in this way with your servants? No straw is given to your servants, and yet they say to us, 'Make bricks.' See how your servants are beaten and how you wrong your people." But he said, "You are lazy, you are lazy; therefore you say, 'Let us go and offer a sacrifice to Jehovah.' Now go and work, for no straw shall be given you; yet you must make the same number of bricks."

Then Moses turned again to Jehovah and said, "Jehovah, why hast thou brought misfortune upon this people? Why is it that thou has sent me? For since I came to Pharaoh to speak in thy name he has wronged this people, and thou hast done nothing at all to rescue thy people."

Jehovah answered Moses, "Now you shall see what I will do to Pharaoh; for compelled by a mighty power he shall surely let them go, and compelled by a mighty power he shall drive them out of his land."

THE COST OF BEING CRUEL AND STUBBORN

Then Jehovah said to Moses, "Pharaoh is stubborn; he will not let the people go. Go to Pharaoh early in the morning, as he is going out on the water, and stand by the bank of the Nile to meet him. Say to him, 'Jehovah, the God of the Hebrews, has sent me to you with this command: Let my people go that they may worship me in the wilderness, but so far you have not listened. Jehovah declares, By this you shall know that I am Jehovah: See, I will strike the waters which are in the river with the rod that is in my hand and they shall be changed into blood. The fish, too, that are in the Nile shall die, and the Nile shall become foul, so that the Egyptians will hate to drink its water.'"

Then Moses lifted up the staff and in the presence of Pharaoh and his servants struck the waters that were in the river Nile; and all its waters were changed into blood. The fish, too, that were in the Nile died, and the river became so foul that the Egyptians could not drink its water, but dug round about the Nile for water to drink.

Seven days later Jehovah gave this command to Moses, "Go in to Pharaoh and say to him, 'Jehovah commands: Let my people go that they may worship me. If you refuse to let them go, then I will afflict all your land with frogs; and the Nile shall swarm with frogs which shall go up and come into your house, into your sleeping chamber, upon your bed, into the houses of your servants, upon your people, and into your ovens and kneading-troughs; and the frogs shall come up even upon you and your people and all your servants.'"

Then Jehovah said to Moses, "Say to Aaron: 'Stretch out your hand with your staff over the rivers, over the canals, and over the pools, and cause frogs to come up over the land of Egypt.'" So Aaron stretched out his hand over the waters of Egypt; and the frogs came up and covered the land of Egypt.

Then Pharaoh called for Moses and Aaron and said, "Pray to Jehovah to take away the frogs from me and my people; then I will let the people go, that they may offer a sacrifice to Jehovah." Moses said to Pharaoh, "Will you do yourself the honor of telling me at what time I shall pray to Jehovah in your behalf and in behalf of your servants and people, that the frogs be destroyed from your palaces and be left only in the Nile?" Pharaoh answered, "To-morrow." Then Moses said, "Let it be as you say; that you may know that there is none like Jehovah our God, the frogs shall depart from you, from your palaces, and from your servants and people; they shall be left only in the Nile."

When Moses and Aaron had gone out from Pharaoh, Moses prayed to Jehovah to remove the frogs which he had brought upon Pharaoh; and Jehovah did as Moses asked. The frogs died in the houses, in the courts, and in the fields, and the people gathered them together in many heaps; and the land was filled with a vile odor. But when Pharaoh saw that relief had come, he was stubborn and, as Jehovah had said, did not listen to Moses and Aaron.

Then Jehovah said to Moses, "Get up early in the morning and stand before Pharaoh, just as he goes out to the water, and say to him, 'Jehovah commands: Let my people go that they may worship me. If you will not let my people go, I will send swarms of flies upon you, upon your servants, and upon your people and into your palaces, so that the houses of the Egyptians shall be full of swarms of flies, as well as the ground upon which they stand. But at that time I will set apart the land of Goshen in which my people live, and no swarms of flies shall be there, so that you may know that I, Jehovah, am in the midst of the earth.'"

And Jehovah did so: a vast swarm of flies came upon Pharaoh's palace and into the homes of his servants; and all the land of Egypt was ruined by the swarms of flies.

Then Pharaoh called for Moses and Aaron and said, "I will let you go that you may offer a sacrifice to Jehovah your God in the wilderness; only you must not go far away. Pray for me." Moses replied, "I will go out and will pray to Jehovah that the swarms of flies may depart from Pharaoh, from his servants and from his people to-morrow; only let not Pharaoh again act deceitfully by refusing to let the people go to offer a sacrifice to Jehovah."

So Moses went out from Pharaoh and prayed to Jehovah. And Jehovah did as Moses asked; but this time also Pharaoh was stubborn and would not let the people go.

Then Jehovah said to Moses, "Go to Pharaoh and tell him, 'Jehovah the God of the Hebrews commands: Let my people go that they may worship me. For if you refuse to let them go and still hold them, then the power of Jehovah will bring a very severe pest upon your cattle which are in the field, upon the horses, the asses, the camels, the herds, and the flocks. But Jehovah will make a difference between the cattle of Israel and the cattle of Egypt, and not one that belongs to the Israelites shall die.'"

So Jehovah set a fixed time, saying, "To-morrow Jehovah will do this in the land." Jehovah did this on the next day, and all the cattle of the Egyptians died; but none of the cattle of the Israelites. Then Pharaoh sent and found that not even one of the cattle of the Israelites was dead; but Pharaoh was stubborn and would not let the people go.

Then Jehovah said to Moses, "Get up early in the morning and stand before Pharaoh, and say to him,'Jehovah, the God of the Hebrews, commands: Let my people go, that they may worship me. Do you still set yourself against my people, so that you will not let them go? To-morrow about this time I will send down a very heavy fall of hail, such as has not been in Egypt from the day that it became a nation until now.'"

So Jehovah sent down hail upon the land of Egypt, and the lightning flashing in the midst of the hail was very severe, such as had not been before in all Egypt since it became a nation. Through the whole land of Egypt the hail struck down everything that was in the field, both man and beast. The hail also struck down all the growing plants and broke all the trees in the fields. Only in the land of Goshen, where the Israelites were, there was no hail.

Again Pharaoh sent and called for Moses and Aaron and said to them, "I have sinned this time; Jehovah is right and I and my people are wrong. Pray to Jehovah, for there has been enough of these mighty thunderings and hail, and I will let you go, and you shall stay no longer." Moses said to him, "As soon as I have gone out of the city, I will spread out my hands in prayer to Jehovah; the thunders shall stop, and there shall be no more hail, that you may know that the earth is Jehovah's. But as for you and your servants, I know that even then you will not fear Jehovah."

So Moses went out of the city from Pharaoh and spread out his hands to Jehovah; and the thunders and hail stopped, and the rain was no longer poured upon the earth. But when Pharaoh saw that the rain and the hail and the thunders had stopped, he sinned again, and he and his servants became stubborn, and he would not let the Israelites go.

So Moses and Aaron went to Pharaoh, and said to him, "Jehovah, the God of the Hebrews, commands: 'How long will you refuse to obey me? Let my people go that they may worship me. For if you refuse to let my people go, then to-morrow I will bring locusts into your land, and they will cover the surface of the earth, so that no one will be able to see the ground, and they shall eat the rest of that which is left to you from the hail, and they shall eat all your trees which grow in the field.'"

Then Moses and Aaron were driven out from Pharaoh's presence, but Moses stretched out his staff over the land of Egypt, and Jehovah caused an east wind to blow over the land all that day and night. In the morning the east wind brought the locusts, and they went over all the land of Egypt and settled down in all the land of Egypt, a very large swarm, more locusts than there ever were before or ever will be again. For they covered the surface of the whole land, so that the land was darkened and nothing green was left, neither tree nor growing plants, anywhere in all the land of Egypt.

Then Pharaoh called for Moses in haste and said, "I have sinned against Jehovah your God and against you. Now therefore forgive my sin only this once, and pray to Jehovah your God to take away from me this deadly plague." So Moses went out from Pharaoh and prayed to Jehovah, and Jehovah made a very strong west wind to blow which took up the locusts and drove them into the Red Sea; not a single locust was left in all the land of Egypt. But Jehovah let Pharaoh's heart remain stubborn, so that he would not let the Israelites go.

Then Jehovah said to Moses, "Stretch out your hand toward heaven, that there may be darkness over the land of Egypt, so dark that it may be felt." So Moses stretched out his hand toward heaven; and there was complete darkness in all the land of Egypt for three days; no one could see another, nor did any one move about for three days. But the Israelites had light in their homes.

Then Pharaoh called Moses and said, "Go, worship Jehovah; only let your flocks and your herds stay behind; let your little ones go with you." But Moses said, "You must also give us animals for sacrifices and burnt-offerings, that we may offer a sacrifice to Jehovah our God. Our cattle too must go with us; not a hoof shall be left behind, for we must take these to offer to Jehovah our God, and we do not know what we must offer to Jehovah until we arrive there."

But Jehovah let Pharaoh's heart remain stubborn, and he would not let them go. And Pharaoh said to him, "Go away from me; take care that you never come to me again; for on the day that you come to me you shall die." Moses replied, "You have spoken truly, I shall never see you again."

Moses said to Pharaoh, "Jehovah declares: 'About midnight I will go through all of Egypt. All the eldest sons in the land of Egypt shall die, from the eldest son of Pharaoh who sits upon his throne, even to the eldest son of the slave girl who is behind the mill, and all the first-born of the cattle. There shall be a great cry of sorrow all over the land of Egypt, such as has never been before and never shall be again.' But not a single dog shall bark at any of the Israelites nor their animals, that you may know that Jehovah does make a difference between the Egyptians and Israelites. All these your servants shall come to me and bow down before me, saying, 'Go away, together with all the people that follow you.' After that I will go away." And Moses went from Pharaoh in great anger.

THE ESCAPE FROM EGYPT

Moses called together all the leaders of Israel, and said to them, "Take lambs from the herds according to your families and kill the passover lamb. You shall also take a bunch of hyssop and dip it in the blood that is in the basin and strike the lintel nd the two door posts withthe blood that is in the basin. And not one of you shall go out of the door of his house until morning, for Jehovah will pass through to kill the Egyptians, and when he sees the blood upon the lintel and on the two door posts, he will pass over the door and will not let the destroyer come into your houses to destroy you. You and your children shall observe this event as a custom forever.

"When your children shall say to you, 'What do you mean by this service?' you shall say, 'It is the sacrifice of the passover of Jehovah, for he passed over the houses of the Israelites in Egypt, when he destroyed the Egyptians and released our people.'"

Then the people bowed their heads and worshipped; and the Israeliteswent and did as Jehovah had commanded Moses and Aaron.

At midnight Jehovah destroyed all the eldest sons in the land of Egypt, from the eldest son of Pharaoh who sat on his throne to the eldest son of the captive who was in prison. Then Pharaoh arose in the night, together with all his servants and all the Egyptians, and there was a great cry of sorrow, for there was not a house in Egypt in which there was not one dead. Pharaoh called Moses and Aaron at night and said, "Go away from among my people, both you and the Israelites; go, worship Jehovah as you have asked. Also take with you your sheep and your cattle, as you have asked, go and ask a blessing for me also." The Egyptians also told the people to hasten out of the land, for they said, "We shall all perish." So the people took their dough before the yeast had worked, and their kneading-troughs were bound up in their clothes upon their shoulders.

The Israelites went on foot from Rameses to Succoth; and a mixed multitude went with them, and they had a great many flocks and herds. They baked unraised cakes of the dough which they had brought with them from Egypt, for there was no yeast in it, because they had been driven out of Egypt and could not wait, neither had they prepared for themselves any food for the journey.

And they went from Succoth and camped at Etham on the border of the wilderness. Jehovah went before them by day in a pillar of cloud, to show them the way, and at night in a pillar of fire, to give them light, that they might march both by day and by night; the pillar of cloud by day and the pillar of fire at night stayed in front of the people.

When the king of Egypt was told that the people had fled, the feeling of Pharaoh and his servants toward them was changed, and they said, "Why have we done this and let the Israelites escape from serving us?" So he made ready his chariot and took his people with him. He also took six hundred chosen chariots and the rest of the chariots of Egypt with captains over all of them; and Jehovah let the heart of Pharaoh, king of Egypt, remain stubborn, so that he followed the Israelites, because they had defied him.

When Pharaoh drew near to them the Israelites looked up and saw the Egyptians marching after them; and they were very much afraid and cried to Jehovah. And they said to Moses, "Why have you misled us by bringing us out of Egypt? Is not this what we told you in Egypt, when we said, 'Let us alone, that we may serve the Egyptians? For it is better for us to serve the Egyptians than to die in the wilderness.'" But Moses said to the people, "Do not be frightened, remain quiet and you will see how Jehovah will save you to-day; for as surely as you now see the Egyptians you shall never see them again. Jehovah will fight for you, and you are to keep still."

Then the angel of God who went before the army of Israel changed his position and went behind them. The pillar of cloud also changed its position from in front of them and stood behind them, coming between the army of the Egyptians and the army of the Israelites. On the one side the cloud was dark and on the other side it lighted up the night, so that throughout all the night neither army came near the other.

Then Moses stretched out his hand over the sea, and Jehovah by means of a strong east wind caused the sea to go back all that night and made the bed of the sea dry. And the Israelites crossed over on the dry bed of the sea. The Egyptians followed and all of Pharaoh's horses, his chariots, and his horsemen went after them into the sea. In the morning before sunrise, Jehovah looked out through the pillar of fire and of cloud upon the army of the Egyptians and threw them into confusion. He also bound their chariot wheels, so that they dragged heavily. Therefore the Egyptians said, "Let us flee from the Israelites, for Jehovah fights for them against us."

Then Jehovah said to Moses, "Stretch out your hand over the sea, that the waters may come back upon the Egyptians, upon their chariots, and upon their horsemen."

So Moses stretched out his hand over the sea, and toward morning the sea returned to its ordinary level while the Egyptians were flying before it. So Jehovah overthrew the Egyptians in the midst of the sea, and the waters returned and covered the chariots and the horsemen, and all the army of Pharaoh that went after them into the sea, so that not one of them was left. Thus Jehovah saved the Israelites that day from the power of the Egyptians; and they saw the Egyptians dead upon the seashore. When the Israelites saw the great work which Jehovah did to the Egyptians, the people feared Jehovah and believed in him and in his servant Moses.

And Miriam the prophetess, the sister of Aaron, took a tambourine in her hand; and as all the women followed her with tambourines and with dancing, she sang with them:

"Sing to Jehovah, for he has triumphed gloriously:
Both horse and rider has he hurled into the sea."

Then Moses and the Israelites sang this song to Jehovah:

"I will sing to Jehovah, for he has triumphed gloriously:
Both horse and rider he has hurled into the sea.
Jehovah is my strength and song, he has delivered me;
He is my God, I will praise him; my father's God whom I honor."

GOD'S COMMANDS TO THE PEOPLE

Moses led the Israelites forward from the Red Sea until they came to the wilderness of Sinai, and there the Israelites camped before the mountain.

Moses went up into the presence of God, and Jehovah called to him from the mountain and said, "Tell the Israelites: 'You have seen what I did to the Egyptians and how I bore you on eagles' wings and brought you to myself. Now therefore, if you will listen to my voice and keep your solemn agreement with me, you shall be my own treasure taken from among all peoples, for all the earth is mine. You shall be a nation of priests, a people devoted to my service.'"

So Moses called together the leaders of the people and told them all these words, as Jehovah had commanded him. And all the people answered together, "We will do all that Jehovah has commanded."

When Moses told Jehovah the answer of the people, Jehovah said to him, "See, I come to you in a thick cloud, that the people may hear when I speak and may always believe in you." And Jehovah said to Moses, "Go to the people and keep them pure to-day and to-morrow, and let them wash their garments and be ready on the third day, for on the third day I will come down on Mount Sinai within sight of all the people."

On the third day, when morning came, there were thunderings and lightnings and a thick cloud rested upon the mountain, and a very loud trumpet blast sounded, so that all the people who were in the camp trembled. Then Moses brought the people out of the camp to meet God; and they stood at the foot of the mountain. Mount Sinai was entirely covered with smoke, because Jehovah came down upon it in fire. And from it smoke went up like the smoke of a furnace, and the entire mountain shook violently.

Then God spoke all these words: "I am Jehovah your God who brought you out of the land of Egypt, from a place where you were slaves.

"THOU SHALT HAVE NO OTHER GODS EXCEPT ME.

"THOU SHALT NOT MAKE FOR THYSELF A GRAVEN IMAGE, nor any image of anything that is in the heavens above, on the earth beneath, or in the waters that are under the earth. Thou shalt not bow down before them, nor serve them, for I Jehovah thy God am a jealous God visiting the sins of the fathers upon the children to the third and fourth generation, but showing acts of kindness to the thousandth generation of those who love me and keep my commands.

"THOU SHALT NOT TAKE THE NAME OF JEHOVAH THY GOD IN VAIN, for Jehovah will not leave him unpunished who takes his name in vain.

"REMEMBER THE SABBATH DAY TO KEEP IT HOLY. Six days shalt thou labor and do all thy work; but the seventh day is the Sabbath of Jehovah thy God. In it thou shalt not do any work, neither thou, nor thy son, nor thy daughter, nor thy male servant, nor thy female servant, nor thy cattle,nor the guest who is with thee, for in six days Jehovah made the heavens and the earth, the sea and all that in them is, and rested on the seventh day. Therefore Jehovah blessed the Sabbath day and made it holy.

"HONOR THY FATHER AND THY MOTHER, that thou mayest live long on the land which Jehovah thy God giveth thee.

"THOU SHALT NOT MURDER.

"THOU SHALT NOT COMMIT ADULTERY.

"THOU SHALT NOT STEAL.

"THOU SHALT NOT BEAR FALSE WITNESS AGAINST THY NEIGHBOR.

"THOU SHALT NOT COVET THY NEIGHBOR'S HOUSE; thou shalt not covet thy neighbor's wife, nor his male servant, nor his female servant, nor his ox, nor his ass, nor anything that belongs to thy neighbor."

Then Jehovah said to Moses, "Write down these words, for in accord with these words I have made a solemn agreement with you and with Israel."

OUR DUTIES TO GOD AND MAN

Hear O Israel: Jehovah our God is the one Lord. You shall love Jehovah your God with all your heart, with all your soul, and with all your strength.

Behold, the heavens, the highest heavens, the earth and all that is on it belong to Jehovah your God. Jehovah showed his love to your fathers more than to any other people, and he has chosen their children after them and you out of all the nations. Therefore, open your heart to him and no longer refuse to be guided by him. For Jehovah your God is God of gods and Lord of lords, the great, the mighty, the wonderful God, who shows no favors and takes no bribes, who sees that what is right is done to the orphan and widow, who loves the foreigner and gives him food and clothing. Love Jehovah your God and always keep his laws and his commands.

You shall not deceive one another.
You shall not lie to one another.
You shall not swear falsely in my name.
You shall not wrong nor rob your neighbor.
You shall not curse the deaf.
You shall not put a stumbling-block before the blind.
You shall not tell stories about one another.
You shall not hate any one.
You shall not take vengeance nor bear a grudge against any one.
You shall love your neighbor as yourself.
You shall rise before the hoary head and honor an old man.

If a foreigner lives in your land, you shall do him no wrong. You shall treat him as one of your own people and you shall love him as yourself.

THE REPORT OF THE HEBREW SPIES

Moses sent certain men to explore the land of Canaan and said to them, "Go up into the South Country and on into the highlands, and see what the land is and whether the people who live there are strong or weak, whether they are few or many, and whether the land in which they live is good or bad, and what kinds of cities they live in, whether in camps or in strongholds. See whether the land is fertile or barren, whether there is wood in it or not. Be courageous and bring some of the fruit of the land," for it was the time when the grapes first begin to ripen.

So they went up to the South Country and came to Hebron. When they came to the valley of Eshcol, they cut down from there a branch with one cluster of grapes and brought it away on a pole carried by two men. They also took some pomegranates and figs. That place was called the valley of the Grape Cluster because of the cluster which the Israelites cut down there.

Then they returned to Moses and Aaron and all the Israelites at Kadesh and brought back word to them and showed them the fruit of the land. They reported to Moses, "We went to the land to which you sent us; and it indeed is full of milk and honey; and this is some of its fruit. But the people who live in the land are strong, and the cities are very large and have high walls about them."

Then Caleb quieted the people and said, "Let us go up at once and take it, for we are well able to conquer it." But the men who had gone up with him said, "We are not able to conquer the people, for they are stronger than we, and all the people whom we saw there are very tall and large. There we saw the giants; we were as grasshoppers in our own sight, and so we seemed to them."

All the people wept that night and cried out, "Why did Jehovah bring us to this land to fall by the sword? Our wives and our little ones will be taken captive. Would it not be better for us to return to Egypt?" So they said to one another, "Let us choose a leader and return to Egypt."

Then Moses and Aaron bowed low before all the Israelites who were gathered there, and Joshua and Caleb, who were among those who explored the land, tore their clothes and said to them, "The land which we went to explore is a very good land. If Jehovah is pleased with us, he will bring us into this land and give it to us, a land which is full of milk and honey. Only do not rebel against Jehovah. Fear not the people of the land, for they will supply us with food. Their defense is taken away from over them, and Jehovah is with us; fear them not." But the people would not trust Jehovah.

Then Jehovah said to Moses, "How long will this people despise me? How long will they refuse to trust me in spite of all of the wonders which I have performed before their eyes? I will send sickness upon them and destroy them, and I will make you and your family a nation greater and mightier than theirs."

But Moses said to Jehovah, "When the Egyptians hear it, they will say, 'Jehovah has killed them in the wilderness because he was not able to bring this people into the land which he solemnly promised to them.' Forgive, I pray thee, the guilt of this people, because thy love is great, even as thou hast forgiven them from the time they left Egypt even until now."

Jehovah said, "I have forgiven as you have asked; but as surely as I live and as surely as the whole earth shall be filled with the glory of Jehovah, none of the men who have seen my glory and my wonders which I performed in Egypt and in the wilderness, and yet have tested me these ten times and have not listened to my voice, shall see the land which I have solemnly promised to their fathers, neither shall any of those who despise me see it. But I will bring my servant Caleb to the land to which he went, for he has shown a different spirit and has faithfully followed me, and his children shall possess it. But your little ones, who, you said, would be captives of war, I will bring in, and they shall possess the land which you have refused. Your dead bodies shall fall in this wilderness, and your children shall be wanderers there forty years and shall suffer for your unfaithfulness until your bodies have all decayed in the wilderness."

THE LAST WORDS OF MOSES

When Moses was old, he said to all the Israelites, "I am a hundred and twenty years old this day. I can no longer go out and come in, and Jehovah has said to me, 'You shall not go over this river Jordan.'

Jehovah your God is going over before you. He will destroy these nations before you, and you shall drive them out; and Joshua is going over to lead you as Jehovah has commanded. Be brave and strong, do not be afraid of them, for Jehovah your God is leading you; he will not fail you nor forsake you."

Moses also called Joshua and said to him in the presence of all Israel, "Be brave and strong, for you shall bring this people into the land which Jehovah has promised to their fathers to give them; and you shall give it to them. Jehovah is going before you; he will be with you, he will not fail nor forsake you; fear not, nor be frightened."

Then Moses went up on the plains of Moab to Mount Nebo to the summit of Pisgah opposite Jericho. And Jehovah showed him all the land, and said to him, "This is the land which I have solemnly promised to Abraham, to Isaac, and to Jacob, saying, 'I will give it to your children.' I have let you see it with your own eyes, but you shall not go over there."

So Moses, the servant of Jehovah, died there in the land of Moab as Jehovah had said. And Jehovah buried him in the deep valley in the land of Moab; but to this day no man knows the place where he was buried. Moses was a hundred and twenty years old when he died, but his eye was not dim nor had he lost his strength. The Israelites wept for Moses on the plain of Moab thirty days, and then the days of weeping and mourning for Moses were ended.

Joshua the son of Nun was filled with the spirit of wisdom, for Moses had laid his hands upon him; and the Israelites listened to him and did as Jehovah commanded Moses. But in Israel no prophet had yet arisen whom Jehovah knew as well as he did Moses.

CROSSING THE RIVER JORDAN

After the death of Moses, Jehovah said to Joshua, Moses' helper, "Moses my servant is dead: Now arise, go over the Jordan with all this people to the land which I am about to give to the Israelites. As long as you live no one will be able to stand against you. As I was with Moses, so I shall be with you: I will not fail you nor forsake you. Be brave and strong, for you shall give this people the land which I solemnly promised their fathers I would give them. Only be brave and strong to keep faithfully all the law, as Moses my servant commanded you. Turn not from it to the right nor to the left, and you shall have success wherever you go. Have I not commanded you? Be brave and strong; fear not nor be afraid, for Jehovah your God is with you wherever you go."

Then Joshua gave this order to the officers who were over the people: "Go through all the camp and give this command: 'Prepare food for yourselves, for within three days you are to cross this Jordan, to go in and take the land which Jehovah your God has given you as your own.'"

While Joshua was at Shittim, he secretly sent two men as spies, with the command: "Go, explore the land and especially Jericho." So they went and entered the house of a woman named Rahab, and stayed there.

It was reported to the king of Jericho, "Some men came here to-night from the Israelites to explore the land." Therefore the king of Jericho sent to Rahab and said, "Bring out the men who entered your house, for they have come to explore all the land."

Now the woman had taken the two men and hidden them; so she said, "It is true, some men came to me, but I did not know where they came from. When the time came to shut the gate at night, the men went out and I do not know where they have gone. Follow after them quickly, for you may overtake them." She, however, had brought them up to the roof and hidden them with the stalks of flax which she had spread out there. So the men of Jericho followed after them in the direction of the fords of the Jordan; and as soon as the men of Jericho had gone out, the gate was closed.

The spies had hardly lain down when Rahab came up to them on the roof and said, "I know that Jehovah has given you the land and that fear of you has seized us and that because of you all who live in the land are losing heart. Now therefore swear to me by Jehovah, since I have treated you with kindness, that you will also treat my family kindly, and promise me that you will save the lives of my father, my mother, my brothers, and my sisters, together with all that they have, and will not put us to death." The men said to her, "We are ready to give our lives for you, if you do not tell what we are doing; and when Jehovah gives us the land, we will treat you kindly and faithfully."

Then she let them down by a rope through the window, for the house in which she lived was built into the city wall. She said to them, "Go into the hills, that the men who are looking for you may not find you, and hide yourselves there three days until they have returned. Then you may go on your way."

The men said to her, "We shall be free from our solemn promise to you, unless, when we come into the land, you bind this cord of scarlet thread in the window through which you let us down and gather your father, your mother, your brothers, and all your family into your house. If any one goes out of the doors of your house into the street, he shall be responsible for his death and we shall be innocent. If any one stays with you in the house, we will be responsible for his death if any one lays hands on him. But if you tell what we are doing, we shall be free from our solemn promise to you." She replied, "It shall be as you say." So she sent them away. And when they were gone, she bound the scarlet cord in the window.

So they left and went into the hills and stayed there three days until those who were looking for them had returned. They sought for them in every direction but did not find them. Then the two men came down from the hills, crossed the river, and came to Joshua and told him all that had happened to them.

Joshua rose up early in the morning and set out from Shittim. And he and all the Israelites came to the Jordan and spent the night there before crossing. And Joshua said to the people, "Consecrate yourselves, for to-morrow Jehovah will do wonders among you. Come and hear the words of Jehovah your God. By this you shall know that a living God is with you: the ark of the Lord of all the earth is about to pass over before you into the Jordan. When the priests who bear the ark of the Lord of all the earth step into the waters of the Jordan, its waters shall be cut off, so that the waters that come down from above will stand still in a heap."

So when the people left their tents to pass over the Jordan, the priests, who were carrying the ark were in front of them. And when the bearers of the ark came to the Jordan, and the feet of the priests who were carrying the ark dipped in the brink of the water--for the Jordan overflows all its banks during the harvest time--the waters that came down from above stood still and its waters rose in a heap a long distance up the river at Adam, the city that is near Zarethan. The waters that went down toward the Dead Sea were wholly cut off, while the people crossed over opposite Jericho. The priests who were carrying the ark of Jehovah stood firm on dry ground in the middle of the Jordan, while all the Israelites passed over on dry ground, until the whole nation had completed the crossing of the Jordan.

When they had all crossed, Jehovah said to Joshua, "Command them to take from the middle of the Jordan, out of the place where the priests' feet stood, twelve stones and carry them over with you and lay them down in the camping-place, where you pass the night, that this may be a reminder to them. Then when your children ask from time to time: 'What do these stones mean to you?' you shall say to them, 'They are reminders that the waters of the Jordan were cut off before the ark of Jehovah, when it passed over the Jordan.' These stones shall be a constant reminder to the Israelites."

So the Israelites did as Joshua commanded and took up out of the middle of the Jordan twelve stones corresponding to the number of the tribes of the Israelites. They carried them over with them to the place where they camped and laid them down there.

Then the waters of the Jordan returned to their place and the river overflowed all its banks as before.

THE CAPTURE OF JERICHO AND AI

Now Jericho had closed its gates because of the Israelites, and no one went in or out. But Jehovah said to Joshua, "See, I have given Jericho to you with its king and its able warriors. You shall march around the city, all the soldiers going about the city once. You shall do this for six days, and on the seventh day the people shall make the attack, each man going up straight before him."

Then Joshua said to the people, "March around the city and let the armed men pass on before the ark of Jehovah. You shall not shout the battle-cry nor let your voice be heard; not a word shall escape from your mouth until the day I say to you, 'Shout the battle-cry'; then you shall shout!"

So he had the ark of Jehovah carried around the city once; then they returned to the camp and spent the night there. The second day they also marched around the city once and returned to the camp. Thus they did six days. The seventh day they rose early at dawn and made the circuit of the city in the same way, only on that day they marched about the city seven times. The seventh time the priests blew the trumpets, and Joshua said to the people, "Shout the battle-cry; for Jehovah has given you the city. The city and all that is in it shall be sacrificed to Jehovah; only Rahab and those who are with her in her house shall live, because she hid the messengers whom we sent."

So the people shouted the battle-cry and the wall fell down and they went straight up into the city and captured it. But Joshua spared the lives of Rahab and her father's family and all that she had, because she hid the messengers whom Joshua sent to explore Jericho; and they have lived among the Israelites even to this day.

Then Joshua set out with all the warriors to go up to Ai. And he selected thirty thousand brave soldiers and sent them out at night with this command, "Hide somewhere beyond the town, not very far from it, but be ready to act. I and all the people who are with me will go toward the town, but when they come out against us, we will flee before them. They will come out after us, until we have drawn them away from the town; for they will say, 'They are fleeing before us.' Then you shall rise up from where you are hiding, and take the town. When you have captured it, set it on fire."

So Joshua sent them out, and they went to the place where they were to hide and placed themselves on the west side of Ai. Joshua spent that night among the people, and rose early the next morning and gathered them, and he went up, together with the rulers of Israel, before the people to Ai. And the warriors who were with him went up and came before the town. When the king of Ai saw it, the men of the town quickly rose up and went out to fight against the Israelites, but the king did not know that men were hiding behind the town to rise up and attack him.

Then Joshua and the Israelites pretended to be beaten and fled toward the wilderness; and all the people that were in the town were called together to pursue them. So they left the town unguarded and pursued the Israelites. Then the men who were hiding rose quickly out of their place and set the town on fire. When the men of Ai looked back, they saw the smoke of the town rising to heaven; and they had no chance to flee this way or that, for the Israelites who had been fleeing to the wilderness turned back upon those who were following them. When the smoke of the town rose up, the rest of the Israelites came out of the town against them; so they were surrounded by the Israelites, some on this side, and some on that, so that they let none of the people of Ai remain or escape.

WOMEN WHO SAVED A NATION

Later Sisera, who had nine hundred iron chariots, cruelly oppressed the Israelites for twenty years. Then the prophetess Deborah, the wife of Lappidoth, delivered Israel. She used to sit under the palm-tree of Deborah between Ramah and Bethel in the highlands of Ephraim; and the Israelites went to her to have her decide their disputes.

She sent and called Barak, the son of Abinoam, from Kadesh Naphtali and said to him, "Does not Jehovah the God of Israel command you: 'Go, march to Mount Tabor and take with you ten thousand of the Naphtalites and of the Zebulunites? Then I will draw out to you at the brook Kishon Sisera with his chariots and his troops, and I will deliver him into your hands.'" Barak said to her, "If you will go with me, I will go, but if you will not go with me, I will not go." She replied, "I will certainly go with you, only you will not have the glory in this expedition on which you are going, for Jehovah will deliver Sisera into the hands of a woman."

So Deborah arose and went with Barak to Kadesh. Barak called the Zebulunites and the Naphtalites together at Kadesh and ten thousand men followed him; and Deborah also went up with him.

Now Heber the Kenite had left the Kenites, the children of Jethro the father-in-law of Moses, and had pitched his tent as far away as the oak which is near Kadesh.

When it was reported to Sisera that Barak the son of Abinoam had gone up to Mount Tabor, Sisera gathered together all his chariots, nine hundred iron chariots, and all his people from the heathen city Harosheth to the brook Kishon. Then Deborah said to Barak, "To the attack! for to-day Jehovah has delivered Sisera into your hands. Has not Jehovah gone out before you?"

So Barak went down from Mount Tabor followed by ten thousand men; and at the attack of Barak's swordsmen Jehovah put to flight Sisera and his chariots and all his forces, and Sisera got down from his war-chariot and fled on foot. But Barak pursued the chariots and the forces to Harosheth; and all the army of Sisera was destroyed by the sword; not a single man was left.

On that day Deborah and Barak, the son of Abinoam, sang this song:

"O Jehovah, when thou wentest from Seir,
Marching from the region of Edom,
Earth trembled, the heavens swayed,
The clouds also dripped water;
The hills quaked before Jehovah,
Yon Sinai, before Israel's God.

"In the days of Anath's son, Shamgar,
In Jael's days the roads were unused,
And travellers walked through byways.
Leaders disappeared in Israel,
Until you, O Deborah, rose,
Till you rose as a mother in Israel.

"My heart is with the commanders of Israel,
Who volunteered among the people. Bless Jehovah!
You who ride on tawny asses,
Who sit upon rich saddle-cloths;
You who walk by the way, tell of it.
Far from sounds of dividing the spoil,
In the places where water is drawn,
Let them tell of Jehovah's righteous acts,
And the righteous deeds of his leaders!

"Then the people of Jehovah
Went down to the gates, crying:

'Awake, awake, O Deborah,
Awake, awake, sing a battle-song!
Rise up, rise up, O Barak,
Take your captives, O son of Abinoam!'

"So they went down against the powerful,
The Lord's people against the mighty.
From Machir, commanders went down,
From Zebulun, standard-bearers,
Issachar's princes with Deborah,
And with Barak, the men of Naphtali;
Into the valley they streamed after him.

"Zebulun risked its life,
Naphtali on the heights of the field.
Rulers came, they fought,
The rulers of Canaan fought
At Taanach by the waters of Megiddo.

"They took no booty of silver,
For from heaven the very stars fought,
From their courses they fought against Sisera.
The brook Kishon swept them away,
That ancient brook, the brook Kishon.
O my soul, march on with strength!
Then did their horse hoofs pound
With the gallop, gallop of steeds.

"Blessed above women shall Jael be,
That wife of Heber, the Kenite,
More blessed than all nomad women!
Water he asked, milk she gave,
Curdled milk she brought him
In a bowl well fitted for lords!
She put her hand to the tent-pin,
Her right hand to the workman's hammer.
She struck Sisera, crushing his head,
She shattered, she pierced his temples.
At her feet he sank down and lay still,
At her feet he sank, he fell;
There he fell, a victim slain!

"Through the window she peered and cried,
Through the lattice, the mother of Sisera:
'Why so long his chariot in coming?
Why tarry the hoof-beats of steeds?'
Then the wisest of her ladies replied,

She herself also answered her question,
'Are they not dividing the spoil?
A woman or two for each warrior,
For Sisera a spoil of dyed stuffs,
A spoil of dyed stuffs embroidered,
Some pieces of lace for his neck?'

"So perish thy foes, O Jehovah!
But may those who love him be as the sun,
Rising up in invincible splendor!"

GIDEON'S BRAVE BAND

In course of time the Midianites conquered the Israelites. To escape them the Israelites made for themselves dens in the mountains and caves and strongholds. When the Israelites had sown their crops, the Midianites would come up and leave nothing for the Israelites to live on, neither sheep, nor ox, nor ass; for they came up with their cattle and their tents. The Israelites were so robbed by the Midianites, that they cried to Jehovah for help.

Then the angel of Jehovah came and sat down under the oak which was in Ophrah that belonged to Joash the Abiezerite; and his son, Gideon, was beating out wheat in the wine-press to hide it from the Midianites. The angel of Jehovah appeared to him and said, "Jehovah is with you, able warrior!" Gideon said to him, "O my lord, if Jehovah is with us, why then has all this overtaken us? Where are all his wonderful acts of which our fathers told us, saying, 'Did not Jehovah bring us from Egypt?' But now Jehovah has cast us off and given us into the power of the Midianites."

Then Jehovah turned to him and said, "With this strength which you have go and save Israel from the rule of the Midianites: do I not send you?" But Gideon said to him, "O Jehovah, how can I save Israel? See, my family is the poorest in Manasseh, and I am the least in my father's house." Jehovah said to him, "I will surely be with you, and you shall overthrow the Midianites as if they were only one man."

Then the spirit of Jehovah took possession of Gideon, and he sounded the war trumpet, and the Abiezerites assembled under his leadership. He also sent messengers throughout all the land of the Manassites, and they assembled under his leadership; and he sent messengers to the Asherites, the Zebulunites, and the Naphtalites, and they went up to join him. But Jehovah said to Gideon, "You have too many people with you; if I give the Midianites up to the Israelites they will boast, 'We have saved ourselves!' Therefore, proclaim to your people, 'Whoever is afraid may go home.'"

Then Gideon separated them, so that twenty-two thousand of the people went back home, but ten thousand stayed. But Jehovah said to him, "The people are still too many; take them down to the water, and I will try them out for you there. Every one of whom I say to you, 'This one shall go with you,' shall go with you; and every one of whom I say to you, 'This one shall not go with you,' shall not go."

So Gideon brought the people down to the water. And Jehovah said to him, "You shall put by themselves all who lap the water with their tongues, as a dog laps, and all who kneel down on their knees to drink by themselves." The number of those who lapped with their tongue, putting their hand to their mouth, were three hundred men; but all the rest of the people knelt down on their knees to drink. Then Jehovah said to Gideon, "By the three hundred men who lapped I will save you and deliver the Midianites into your hands. Let all the rest of the people go home." So they took the food that the people had in their hands, and their trumpets; and Gideon sent home all the other Israelites, keeping only the three hundred men.

Then Gideon came to the Jordan and crossed it, and the three hundred men were with him, faint yet pursuing. And he said to the men of Succoth, "Give, I beg of you, loaves of bread to the people who follow me, for they are faint and I am pursuing after Zebah and Zalmunna, the kings of Midian." But the rulers of

Succoth said, "Are Zebah and Zalmunna already in your power that we should give bread to your band?" Gideon replied, "When Jehovah has delivered Zebah and Zalmunna into my power, for this insult I will thrash your bare flesh with desert thorns and briers." He went on from there to Penuel and made the same request of the men of Penuel, but they made the same answer as the men of Succoth. To the men of Penuel he also said, "When I come back victorious, I will break down this tower."

Zebah and Zalmunna were in Karkor, and their forces were with them, in all about fifteen thousand men. Gideon went up by the caravan road and surprised the horde as it was encamped with no fear of being attacked. He divided the three hundred men into three companies. Into the hands of all of them he put horns and empty earthen jars. In each jar was a torch. He also said to them, "Watch me and do as I do. When I reach the outside of the camp and those who are with me blow a blast on the horn, then you also shall blow your horns on every side of the camp and cry, 'For Jehovah and Gideon!'"

So Gideon and the hundred men with him reached the outside of the camp at the beginning of the middle watch, when guards had just been posted; and they blew the horns and broke in pieces the jars that were in their hands. The two other companies also broke their jars, took the torches in their left hands and their swords in their right, and cried, "The Sword of Jehovah and of Gideon." And as they stood where they were, about the camp, the entire horde awoke, sounded the alarm, and fled. Zebah and Zalmunna also fled; but Gideon followed and captured the two kings of Midian and threw all the horde into a panic.

When Gideon returned from the battle, he captured a young man who lived at Succoth. At Gideon's request he wrote down for him the names of the rulers of Succoth and its leading men. There were seventy-seven in all. When Gideon came to the men of Succoth, he said, "See, here are Zebah and Zalmunna about whom you mocked me, saying, 'Are Zebah and Zalmunna already in your power that we should give bread to your men who are weary?'" Then he took desert thorns and briers, and with these he thrashed the leading men of Succoth. He also broke down the tower of Penuel and put to death the men of the town.

Then Gideon said to Zebah and Zalmunna, "What kind of men were those whom you killed at Tabor?" They replied, "They were just like you; each of them looked like a prince." Gideon said, "They were my own brothers, the sons of my mother. As surely as Jehovah lives, if you had saved them alive, I would not kill you now."

Then he said to Jether, his oldest son, "Up and kill them." But the boy did not draw his sword, because he was afraid, for he was only a boy. Then Zebah and Zalmunna said, "Get up yourself and fall upon us; for a man has a man's strength!" So Gideon rose and killed Zebah and Zalmunna, and took the crescents that were on their camels' necks.

Then the men of Israel said to Gideon, "Rule over us, and not only you but your son and your son's son after you, for you have saved us from the power of the Midianites." Gideon said to them, "I will not rule over you, nor shall my son rule over you; Jehovah shall rule over you; but let me make one request of you: let every man give me the ear-rings from his spoil" (for they had golden ear-rings, because they were desert dwellers). They answered, "Certainly, we will give them." So they spread out a blanket and each man threw into it the ear-rings from his spoil. The weight of the golden ear-rings for which he had asked was nearly seventy pounds of gold. Then Gideon made of the gold a priestly robe to wear when asking questions of Jehovah, and placed it in his own city, Ophrah.

Gideon died at a good old age and was buried in the tomb of Joash, his father, in Ophrah of the Abiezerites.

JEPHTHAH'S FOOLISH PROMISE

Jephthah, the Gileadite, was an able warrior, but he was the son of awicked
woman, and had fled from his relatives and lived in the land of Tob. There certain
rascals gathered about him, and they used to go out on raids with him.

After a time the Ammonites made war against the Israelites. Then the elders of
Gilead went to bring Jephthah from the land of Tob, and they said to him, "Come
and be our commander, that we may fight against the Ammonites." But Jephthah
said to the elders of Gilead, "Are you not the men who hated me and drove me out
of my father's house? Why then do you come to me now when you are in trouble?"
But the elders of Gilead said to Jephthah, "This is why we have now turned to you,
that you may go with us and fight against the Ammonites, and you shall be our
chief, even over all the people who live in Gilead." Then Jephthah said to the
rulers of Gilead, "If you take me back to fight against the Ammonites and Jehovah
gives me the victory over them, I shall be your chief." The elders of Gilead replied,
"Jehovah shall be a witness between us; we swear to do as you say."

Then Jephthah went with the elders of Gilead, and the people made him chief and
commander over them. Jephthah also made this vow to Jehovah: "If thou wilt
deliver the Ammonites into my power, then whoever comes out of the door of my
house to meet me, when I return victorious fromthe Ammonites, shall be Jehovah's,
and I will offer that one as an offering to be burned with fire."

So Jephthah went out to fight against the Ammonites; and Jehovah gave him the
victory over them, and delivered them into his hands. But when he came home to
Mizpah, his daughter was just coming out to meet him with tambourines and

choral dances. She was his only child; besides this one he had neither son nor daughter. So when he saw her, he tore his clothes and said, "Oh, my daughter, you have stricken me! It is you who are the cause of my woe! for I have made a solemn vow to Jehovah and cannot break it." She said to him, "My father, you have made a solemn vow to Jehovah; do to me what you have promised, since Jehovah has punished your enemies the Ammonites. But let this favor be granted me: spare me two months that I may go out upon the mountains with those who would have been my bridesmaids and lament because I will never become a wife and mother." He said, "Go."

So he sent her away for two months with her friends, and she mourned on the mountains because she would never become a wife and mother. At the end of two months she returned to her father, who did what he had vowed to do, even though she had never been married. So it became a custom in Israel: each year the women of Israel go out for four days to bewail the death of the daughter of Jephthah, the Gileadite.

SAMSON WHO DID TO OTHERS AS THEY DID TO HIM

There was a certain man of Zorah, of the clan of the Danites, named Manoah; and he and his wife had no children. But the angel of Jehovah appeared to the woman and said to her, "See, you have no children; but now be careful not to drink any wine nor strong drink, and do not eat anything unclean, for you are about to have a son. No razor shall be used upon your son's head, for from birth the boy shall belong to God." So the woman had a son and named him Samson.

Once Samson went down to Timnah and saw there a Philistine woman. When he came back he said to his father and mother, "I have seen a Philistine woman in Timnah. Get her as a wife for me." But his father and mother said to him, "Is there no woman in your own tribe or among all our people, that you must marry a wife from among the heathen Philistines?" But Samson said to his father, "Get her for me, for she suits me."

So Samson went with his father and mother to Timnah; and just as they came to the vineyards of Timnah, a full-grown young lion came roaring toward him. The spirit of Jehovah came upon Samson and, although he had nothing in his hand, he tore the beast in two as one tears a kid. But he did not tell his father and mother what he had done.

Then he went down and talked with the woman, and she suited him. When he returned after a while to marry her, he turned aside to see what was left of the lion, and there was a swarm of bees and honey in the carcass. He scraped the honey out into his hands and went on, eating it as he went. When he came to his father and mother, he gave some to them, and they ate; but he did not tell them that he had taken the honey out of the carcass of the lion.

Then Samson went down to the woman; and he gave a feast there (for so bridegrooms used to do). When the Philistines saw him, they provided thirty comrades to be with him. And Samson said to them, "Let me now tell you a riddle. If you can tell me what it is within the seven days of the feast, I will give you thirty fine linen robes and thirty suits of clothes; but if you cannot tell me, then you shall give me thirty fine linen robes and thirty suits of clothes." They said to him, "Tell your riddle, that we may hear it." And he said to them:

> "Out of the eater came something to eat,
> And out of the strong came something sweet."

But for six days they could not solve the riddle.

On the seventh day they said to Samson's wife, "Tease your husband until he tells us the riddle, or else we will burn up you and your father's house. Did you invite us here to make us poor?" So Samson's wife wept before him and said, "You only hate me and do not love me at all! You have told a riddle to my fellow countrymen and not told me what it is." He said to her, "See, I have not told it to my father or my mother, and shall I tell you?" So she wept before him as long as their feast lasted, but on the seventh day he told her, because she kept asking him; and she told the riddle to her fellow countrymen.

So the men of the city said to him on the seventh day before the sun went down, "What is sweeter than honey? And what is stronger than a lion?" And he said to them:

"If with my heifer you did not plough,
You had not solved my riddle now."

Then he was suddenly given divine strength, and he went down to Ashkelon and killed thirty of their men and took the spoil from them and gave the suits of clothes to those who had guessed the riddle. But he was very angry and returned to his father's house. And his bride was given to his comrade who had been his best man.

After a while, at the time of wheat harvest, Samson went to visit his wife with a kid as a present; but when he said, "Let me go into the inner room to my wife," her father would not let him go in, but said, "I thought that you must surely hate her, so I gave her to your best man. Is not her younger sister fairer than she? Take her then, instead." But Samson said to him, "This time I shall be justified if I do the Philistines an injury." So he went and caught three hundred foxes, turned them tail to tail, and put a torch between every pair of tails. When he had set the torches on fire, he let them go into the standing grain of the Philistines and burned up not only the shocks and the standing grain, but the olive orchards as well.

Then the Philistines said, "Who has done this?" The reply was, "Samson, the son-in-law of the Timnite, because that man took Samson's wife and gave her to his best man." So the Philistines went up, and burnt her and her father. Then Samson said to them, "If this is the way you do, I will not stop until I have had my revenge on you!" So he fought fiercely and killed many of them; then he went and stayed in a cavern in the cliff of Etam.

When the Philistines went up and camped in Judah and made a raid on Lehi, the Judahites said, "Why have you come up against us?" They replied, "We have come up to bind Samson, to do to him what he has done to us." Then three thousand men of Judah went down to the cavern in the cliff of Etam and said to Samson, "Do you not know that the Philistines are our rulers? What are you doing to us?" He replied, "I have done to them as they did to me." They said to him, "We have come down to bind you, to turn you over to the Philistines." Samson said to them, "Swear to me that you will not attack me yourselves." They said to him, "No; we will simply bind you securely and deliver you to them; but we will not kill you." So they bound him with two new ropes, and brought him up from the cliff.

When he came to Lehi, the Philistines shouted when they met him. Then he was suddenly given divine strength, and the ropes that were on his arms became like flax that has been burned in the fire, and his bonds melted from his hands. And he found a fresh jaw-bone of an ass, and having seized it, he killed a thousand men with it. Then Samson said:

"With the jaw-bone of an ass have I piled them, mass on mass;
A thousand warriors have I slain with the jaw-bone of an ass."

A STRONG MAN WHO LOST HIS STRENGTH

Afterward, Samson fell in love with a woman in the valley of Sorek, named Delilah. Then the rulers of the Philistines came to her and said, "Find out by teasing him how it is that his strength is so great and how we may overpower and bind him that we may torture him. Then we will each one of us give you eleven hundred pieces of silver." So Delilah said to Samson, "Tell me how it is that your strength is so great and how you might be bound to torture you?" Samson said to her, "If they should bind me with seven green bowstrings which have not been dried, I would become weak like any other man."

Then the rulers of the Philistines brought her seven green bowstrings which had not been dried, and she bound him with them. She had the men lying in wait in the inner room, but when she said to him, "The Philistines are upon you, Samson!" he snapped the bowstrings as a piece of yarn is snapped when it comes near the fire; so they did not find out the secret of his strength.

Then Delilah said to Samson, "You have deceived me and lied to me; now tell me with what you can be bound fast." He said to her, "If they should bind me securely with new ropes with which no work has been done, I would become weak like any other man." So Delilah took new ropes and bound him with them and said to him, "The Philistines are upon you, Samson!" Men were also lying in wait in the inner room; but he snapped the ropes from his arms like thread.

Again Delilah said to Samson, "So far you have deceived me and lied to me; tell me now with what you can be bound fast." He said to her, "If you should weave the seven braids on my head along with the web and beat it into form with the weaving pin, I would become weak like any other man." So while he was asleep, she took the seven braids of his hair and wove it with the web and beat it into form with the pin, and said to him, "The Philistines are upon you, Samson!" But he awoke out of his sleep and pulled up the loom and the web.

Then she said to him, "How can you say, 'I love you,' when you do not trust me? You have deceived me three times already and have not told me the secret of your great strength." But in time, since she daily begged and urged him, he was wearied to death, and told her all that he knew, saying, "A razor has never touched my head; for I have belonged to God from my birth. If I should be shaved, my strength would be gone, and I would become weak like any other man."

When Delilah saw that he had told her all that he knew, she sent and called for the rulers of the Philistines and said, "Come at once, for he has told me all that he knows." Then the rulers of the Philistines came up to her and brought the money with them. After she had put Samson to sleep on her knees, she called for a man and had him shave off the seven braids on his head. Then she began to tease him, and his strength went from him; and she said, "The Philistines are upon you, Samson!" And he awoke out of his sleep and thought, "I will get up as I have done at other times and shake myself free"; for he did not know that Jehovah had left him. So the Philistines seized him and bored out his eyes. Then they brought him down to Gaza and bound him with chains of brass, and then he was set to grinding in the prison. But the hair of his head began to grow again as soon as he was shaved.

Then the rulers of the Philistines assembled to offer a great sacrifice to their god Dagon and to rejoice, for they said, "Our god has given Samson, our enemy, into our power." When the people saw him, they also praised their god, saying:

"Our god has laid low our foe,
He who brought our country woe,
He who slew us with many a blow."

When they were in high spirits, they said, "Call Samson that he may amuse us." So they called Samson from the prison and he amused them; and they placed him between the pillars. Then Samson said to the young man who held him by the hand, "Let me touch the pillars on which the building rests, that I may lean against them." Now the building was full of men and women, and all the rulers of the Philistines were there, and on the roof about three thousand men and women were looking on while Samson amused them. Samson called on Jehovah and said, "O Jehovah, remember me and strengthen me, I pray thee, just this once, O God, that by one act I may avenge myself on the Philistines for the loss of my two eyes."

Then Samson took hold of the two middle pillars upon which the building rested, one with his right hand and the other with his left, and leaned against them. And Samson said, "Let me die with the Philistines." Then he bent over with all his strength, and the house fell upon the rulers and upon all the people who were in it. So those whom he killed at his death were more than those whom he killed during his lifetime. Then his brothers and all his family came down and took him away and buried him between Zorah and Eshtaol in the burying-place of Manoah his father.

www.ingramcontent.com/pod-product-compliance
Lightning Source LLC
Chambersburg PA
CBHW081158090426

42736CB00017B/3374